# NUMERIC HARMONY

## *2023 NUMBERSCOPES*

## Deborah Breeland

**Independently Published**

To everyone who can or wishes to hear the
one song the UNI-Verse is singing.

*"If you want to find the secrets of the universe think in terms
of energy, frequency, and vibration."*

*Nikola Telsa*

# CONTENTS

# WHAT IS NUMERIC HARMONY?

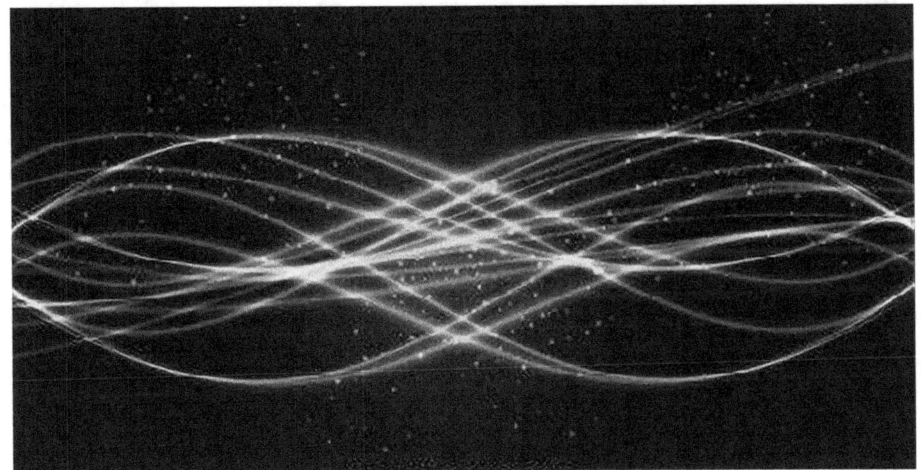

Numeric Harmony is a voice in the universe that contributes to the beautiful melody that is heard when true harmony is achieved. The ONE SONG then becomes clear to any who hears it. A composition of notes, unique voices, and frequencies all woven together. The Uni-Verse sings it constantly, there are different ways and tools to use to amplify and hear it. Numeric Harmony is one way, using the energy and vibration of numbers.

The Greek Philosopher Pythagoras believed that each number carried a certain unique energy or vibration and that each one was associated with different traits or aspects. Continuing that same concept, each number also has varying frequency or tone, like the lower base tones, subtle and underlying, more felt than heard.

Then there are the melodious mid-range tones more mellow and soothing and the high-pitched tone, like the sound that only dogs hear, intense and hyper.

Each number has a full range of ways its traits can manifest and be expressed depending on the frequency or tone. Nikola Tesla said, "If you wanted to know the secrets of the universe, think in terms of energy, vibration, and frequency." After studying Numerology for many years, I agree.

# WHAT IS A NUMBERSCOPE?

Everybody knows what a Horoscope is, it is a forecast of current events based on your astrological sun sign and the alignment of the planets in the heavens now. Well, a Numberscope is much the same thing but instead of using the planets, it is compiled from the numbers that make up the date, all the numbers (MM/DD/YYYY).

In much the same way as a horoscope does, it is possible to look at the total and the numbers that make up that total to get a forecast of current events. Unlike the information gotten from the planets The Numberscope is generic, instead of personal, it is valid for everyone because it is the vibration of the date whether it is in the USA or Egypt or if you are a Leo or a Scorpio. The Numberscope is for everyone.

Just to clarify, the entire date is added up and the total sum is then reduced to a single digit. Adding one number to the next until you get your total which is usually a double-digit number, add those digits in the same manner until you only have a single-digit number. The only exception is with Master numbers 11, 22, 33, and 44. Master Numbers carry higher energy or vibration, you should never reduce master numbers appearing as stand-alone numbers, always add these as 11, 22, 33, or 44.

For example, the date 9/22/2022 would add as 9+22= 31+2= 33+ 0= 33+2= 35+2= 37 total 3+7= 10 1+0= 1

$$9 - 22 - 2022 = 37 / 10 / 1$$

*That date is a 1 which says that the tone of that day is about standing on your own, independence, and new starts. The other numbers in this date say that there may be issues dealing with communication or expression along with issues regarding trust that you will need to deal with. Anytime you start new things you need to let go of other things.*

*Embedded within this date are two Master Numbers, the 22 of the day and the 22 of the year. This says that you will have to be organized, stable, and put in some effort on whatever new you are stepping into for it to work. The keyword for this day is structure.*

This numberscope looks at the entire date and incorporates every vibration of every number in varying frequencies depending on where they appear in the date.

# USING THIS INFORMATION IN YOUR LIFE

Based on today's date, this NUMBERSCOPE indicates the harmonic vibration of this day so you can work with the tone of the day to your best advantage.

This is the statement that appears on every NUMBERSCOPE that I do. One of the reasons why I named my first book Numeric Harmony was because I heard the song of the numbers and I learned that if you paid attention to the vibration and frequency of the numbers that you are looking at, you could hear the harmony and it did make sense to work WITH that energy instead of working against it.

Not every NUMBERSCOPE is going to hit home, most do, but not always. I have found that it is so much better to be forewarned than to have things thrust at us unannounced and out of the blue. With most NUMBERSCOPES, there is some sort of caution, something that should be avoided on that day. Again, not always going to present but as I indicated forearmed is a good thing.

I know that if you are aware of the vibrations then you sometimes make different choices, that is most definitely experience speaking. So, to answer the question. How can you use this information in your life? It could be that you show compassion where you may not have normally, or spoke your truth when necessary, or maybe just take a minute to look into your heart when that is needed. A small thing or a gigantic thing is good and anytime you can sync with the energy it is a WIN-WIN situation as I see it.

Having a full year of NUMBERSCOPES is beneficial, you can look ahead to see what energies may be prominent and plan events that work with the daily energy. Or maybe look back at recent NUMBERSCOPES and remem ber what was going on at that time. See the synchronicity of the energy and how you could have, maybe, handled things differently, by not allowing low vibes present to take control. Looking back, after the fact, you may see patterns and influences that you were unaware of at the time.

Sometimes hindsight really is 20-20

In numerology, there are only 9 numbers to look at and pull information from using only the vibration of each number. Using the frequency opens up a whole spectrum  of other traits ranging from the low, deep subconscious tones to a high, intense super-conscious tone and all tones in between.

In the 365 days of an entire year, there will be repetition, but I believe that you will see the change in the tone depending on the numbers in the date. On Facebook, I am still posting my daily NUMBERSCOPE to a few different pages. On Facebook look for #dailynumericharmony or #numberscope. Follow me on Facebook @Deborah Breeland, to get the NUMBERSCOPE daily, as I post them.

# THIS YEAR
## 2023 IS A
## 7

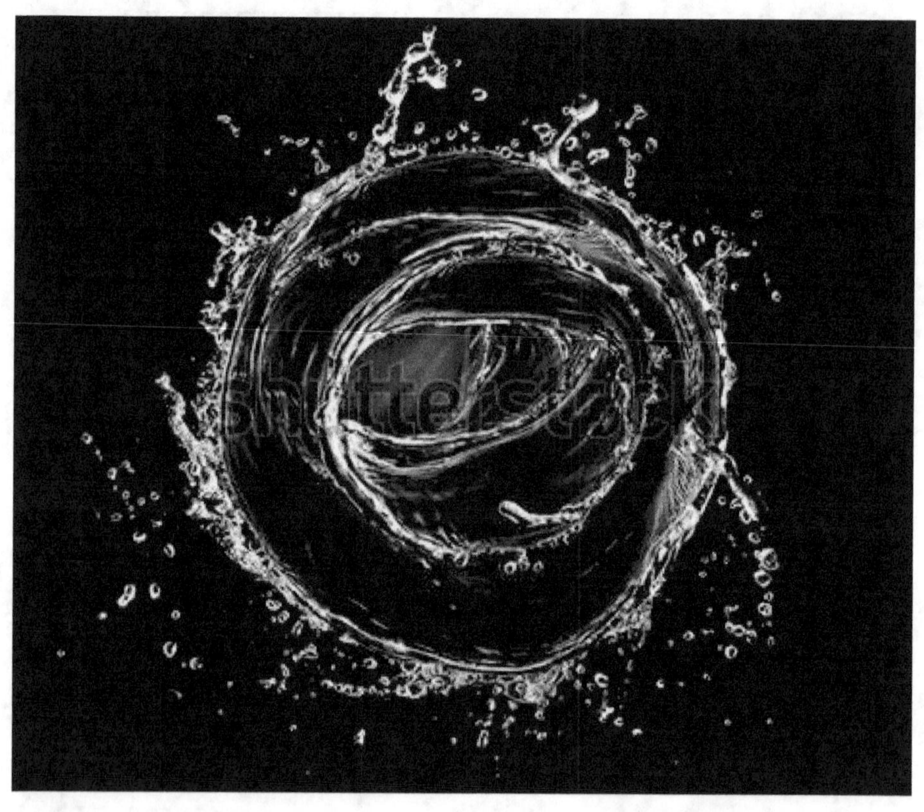

This 7 says that this entire year is all about knowing yourself, trusting your intuition, and gaining knowledge. You may see opportunities come up that will test your knowledge of yourself and what you really want. You may need to learn to be alone, but not lonely. Essentially learn to be happy with your own company. You will be looking within, seeing what is there, and learning to trust what you find.

Trust issues will be ever-present so learn to look within, to feel, and decern your answer, it is like your own 'lie detector'. With this built-in model, you have to learn to trust the results. How many times do you need to hear yourself say "I should have gone with my first instinct"?

There may be some sort of formal education this year, or at the least supplemental classes that teach specific skills. Try to curb your tendency to be skeptical, cynical, or sarcastic, and avoid isolation. Something that you believe in strongly may fall from grace temporarily, do not lose faith. It is a good year for introspection and giving trust another try. This year will test your faith and may redefine your own spiritually, be open and accepting, trust but verify, always.

# 2023 JANUARY

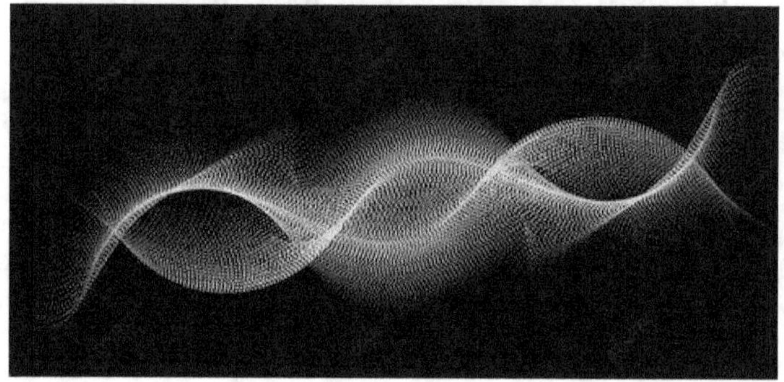

This is a 1 month which says that the introspection influence of the year will be complemented by this 1, bringing independence, idealism, inventiveness, and new beginnings. January will be a time to grab any new venture that presents itself to you. Be aware that lower and even higher vibrations will cycle through occasionally. Watch out for insecurity, inpatients, and ego. Entertain the possibility of thinking outside the box and maybe creating something unique and different. This is pure 1 energy that brings strong independence and inventiveness all month long.

# JANUARY WEEK ONE - 1 THRU 7

**1 / 1 / 2023 = 9**

This day says that we are closing one chapter and opening another. generosity, compassion, and charity will win the day. The keyword is independence.

**1 / 2 / 2023 = 10 / 1**

This day says that we are moving forward looking for new starts, and new beginnings. A strong need to keep your balance and guard your independence. The keyword is tact.

**1 / 3 / 2023 = Master Number 11**

This day says that stakes are being raised, instead of just being about you, this day is about the many, what you say today could have a far-reaching effect. The keyword is communication.

**1 / 4 / 2023 = 12 / 3**

This day says that communication,  expression, and sensitivity will be important today. Try not to be thrown off balance by the words or actions of another. The keyword is stability.

## 1 / 5 / 2023 - 13 / 4

This day says that structure, organization, and work will have an influence and that you should watch how you express yourself. The keyword is change.

## 1 / 6 / 2023 = 14 / 5

This day says that physical activity, change, and personal freedom are at the forefront. Pay special attention at work, things may be chaotic, and try not to show that stubborn side. The keyword is commitment.

## 1 / 7 / 2023 = 15 / 6

This day says that responsibility, commitment, and service to others is the tone today. Avoid overtaxing yourself physically. The keyword is trust.

# JANUARY WEEK TWO
# - 8 THRU 14

**1 / 8 / 2023 = 16 / 7**

This day says that gaining knowledge, looking within, and trust are the main elements of today. take care not to over-commit. The keyword is management.

**1 / 9 / 2023 = 17 / 8**

This day says that power, authority, and money are important, and will be present today in some form. There is the possibility of blindly trusting, be sure to get all the facts. The keyword is compassion.

**1 / 10 / 2023 = 9**

This day says that wisdom, closure, and compassion are the focus today. Think about all the new that is on the horizon and use wisdom and compassion to close what is no longer serving you. The keyword is innovation.

**1 / 11 / 2023 = 19 / 10 / 1**

This day says that inventiveness, innovation, and independence, are at the forefront. But your idealistic nature can be a detriment occasionally. The keyword is teaching.

## 1 / 12/ 2023 = Master Number 11

This day says that the energy of the Master Teacher is presently bringing the opportunity of being in the limelight, either before a small group or from a podium. The keyword is expression.

## 1 / 13 / 2023 = 12 / 3

This day says that creativity, expression, and sensitivity, have the most energetic pull. Express yourself, create beauty, and allow your sensitive side to shine. The keyword is transformation.

## 1 / 14 / 2023 = 13 / 4

This day says that stability, foundation, and structure are the focus. Lay a strong foundation so your structure has stability. The keyword is physical activity.

# JANUARY WEEK THREE - 15 THRU 21

**1 / 15 / 2023 = 14 / 5**

This day says that imagination, change, and freedom are the energies present. Changes are coming, use your imagination to see changes that give you the freedom to do what you like. The keyword is love.

**1 / 16 / 2023 = 15 / 6**

This day says that commitment, responsibility, and love are the things to focus on today. consider making that commitment, or take responsibility, or maybe declare your love. The keyword is to look within.

**1 / 17 / 2023 = 16 / 7**

This day says that trust, faith, and a need to believe are high on the list. You tend to love deeply and sometimes trust blindly. I am not saying don't trust, trust, just verify. The keyword is authority.

**1 / 18 / 2023 = 17 / 8**

This day says that money, power, and management are the focus. Managing time, money and people will go a long way toward establishing your power. Be careful whom you trust. The keyword is generosity.

**1 / 19 / 2023 = 18 / 9**

This day says that charity, compassion, and ancient wisdom will be on board. Use your compassion to distribute charity to those in need. Acknowledge the innate wisdom that you carry. The keyword is idealism.

**1 / 20 / 2023 = 10 / 1**

This day says that independence, standing on your own, and speaking your truth are what is going to be important. Keep your eyes open for that new beginning or a fresh start and maintain your balance.The keyword is nurturing.

**1 / 21 / 2023 = Master Number 11**

This day says that Master Teacher influences are front and center bringing high vibration energy. You may be experiencing it as a more mundane 2 more about personal balance and using tact than about teaching mankind. The keyword is sensitivity.

# JANUARY WEEK FOUR - 22 THRU 28

**1 / 22 / 2023 = 30 / 3**

This day says that sensitivity and expression will be leading the way, communicate your desires but do not be influenced by your feelings. Try expressing yourself dispassionately. The keyword today is to build a strong foundation.

**1 / 23 / 2023 = 13 / 4**

This day says that structure, stability, and work are the focus today, you value these traits in your work environment, try applying them in your life. Transition is coming, make it meaningful. The keyword is change.

**1 / 24 /2023 = 14 / 5**

This day says that change, excess, and imagination are going to be important today. Pay attention to how things present themselves, order will be significant. The keyword is commitment.

**1 / 25 / 2023 = 15 / 6**

This day says that responsibility, commitment, and love  will rule this period. Avoid excesses or restless change. Go with your heart, not a whim or wild hair. The keyword is trust.

**1 / 26 / 2023 = 16 / 7**

This day says that learning new things about yourself and others is on the agenda right now. While still taking in the new aspect also strive to understand the old. The keyword is power.

**1 / 27 / 2023 = 17 / 8**

This day says that authority, management, and power will be in the mix. You may be asked to trust but do not do that blindly, always verify. The keyword is compassion.

**1 / 28 / 2023 = 18 / 9**

This day says that dynamics, impulse, and motivation will all show up. Things are intense, check all your sources. The keyword is stand on your own.

# JANUARY  WEEK FIVE
# - 29 THRU 31

**1 / 29 / 2023 = 19 /10 / 1**

This day says that independence, new starts, and inventiveness are definitely at play. Things stopping and starting, taking in everything in between. The keyword is to learn.

**1 / 30 / 2023 = Master Number 11**

This day says that everything is raised to a higher level, balance, tact, learning, and advice. Be careful to stand your ground and speak your truth because others are listening. The keyword is action.

**1 / 31 / 2023 = 12 / 3**

This day says that communication, feelings, and self-expression are all paramount. Maintaining your balance, and staying centered will help. The keyword is organization.

# 2023 FEBRUARY

This is a 2 month which says that regardless of the other numbers in the date there is a need to maintain your balance and seek your personal center. Basically, keep yourself on an even keel this month. Nurture those near you, and exercise tact with all your interactions. There will be some emotional issues coming up, maybe indecision or feeling victimized, lies or untruths, those are all lower vibration 2 energy, Try regaining your balance, it will help dispel the 2's blues.

# FEBRUARY WEEK ONE - 1 THRU 7

**2 / 1 / 2023 = 10 / 1**

This day says that innovation, industrious deeds, and an inventive mindset all are at the mark, waiting for the signal to go. There are new beginnings coming so make the best of them. The keyword is stand tall.

**2 / 2 / 2023 = MASTER NUMBER 11**

This day says that balance and centering is the focus, with the month and the day both reflecting the same number. Master Number 11 is putting pressure on speaking your truth. The keyword is nurturing self.

**2 / 3 / 2023 = 12 / 3**

This day says that sensitivity, expression, and communication will be present in many different aspects, avoid being caught off guard because it will set you back. The keyword is to socialize.

**2 / 4 / 2023 = 13 / 4**

This day says that work, organization, structure, and stability are what will present looking for attention. See what needs doing and do it, no discussion is necessary. The keyword is practicality.

**2 / 5 / 2023 = 14 / 5**

This day says that imagination, physical effort, and excesses are the energies that are prominent. Do not show your stubborn side and avoid chaos. The keyword is freedom.

**2 / 6 / 2023 = 15 / 6**

This day says that love, service to others, and responsibility will be at the forefront asking for commitment. Be careful with those long terms, remember, you get restless. The keyword is tenacity.

**2 / 7 / 2023 = 16 / 7**

This day says that faith, knowledge, and trust are leading the energy charge, you may be asked to define your spirituality. Knowing your truth and trusting your insight will have a bearing on the answer you give, The keyword is introspection.

# FEBRUARY WEEK TWO - 8 THRU 14

**2 / 8 / 2023 = 17 / 8**

This day says that management, power, and karma are the prominent energies. It is important to look within and trust what you find. Regain your power by dispelling karma (see afterword). The keyword is authority.

**2 / 9 / 2023 = 18 / 9**

This day says that impulse, dynamics, and charity are on the table and will need to be dealt with. Acting on impulse will get you in trouble Apply personal dynamic to  your favorite cause. The keyword is generosity.

**2 / 10 / 2023 = 19 / 10 / 1**

This day says that independence, innovation, and forward vision are the focus. See change as an outstanding opportunity and do not allow ego to color it, Spin the wheel and take a chance. The keyword is new beginnings.

**2 / 11 / 2023 = 20 / 2**

This day says that persuasion, tact, and nurturing are all involved here. Be sure not to be shy or indecisive when interacting with others The keyword is mentor.

**2 / 12 / 2023 = 12 / 3**

This day says that popularity, sensitivity, and reservation are the energies people are responding to. No time to be shy, be the social butterfly. Sometimes being reserved and sensitive is very alluring. The keyword is self-expression.

**2 / 13 / 2023 = 13 / 4**

This day says that practical issues, organization, and structure will all be called for. Try not to become scattered or blocked, pull upon that strong work ethic. The keyword is organization.

**2 / 14 / 2023 = 14 / 5**

This day says that adventure, change, and excess are the most prominent energies at work. Explore, expect changes, and do not overdo it. The keyword is restless.

# FEBRUARY WEEK THREE
## - 15 THRU 21

**2 / 15 / 2023 = 15 / 6**

This day says that infatuation, responsibility, and tenacity are presenting themselves. Avoid being restless, excessive, and moody. The keyword is domestic harmony.

**2 / 16 / 2023 = 16 / 7**

This day says that analytics, sarcasm, and being cynical are energies you may see or feel. These are all lower vibes, which means your personal vibration is too low, do exercises to raise it. The keyword is knowledge.

**2 / 17 / 2023 = 17 / 8**

This day says that authority, having power, and managing that power is prominent. Trust may be an issue, seek your inner resources. The keyword is finance.

**2 / 18 / 2023 = 18 / 9**

This day says that impulse, charity, and compassion are the energies you will feel most. Avoid jealousy or revenge. The keyword is karma.

**2 / 19 / 2023 = 19 / 10 / 1**

This day says that taking chances, starting new, and standing on your own are the things that are prominent. do not be impulsive or selfish. The keyword is impromptu.

**2 / 20 / 2023 = MASTER NUMBER 11**

This day says that teaching, mentoring, and advising are on the table, you will be asked for your advice, help or knowledge, and share it freely. You never know who you may be touching. The keyword is nurturing.

**2 / 21 / 2023 = 12 / 3**

This day says that socializing, being popular, and expressing yourself will be important. Travel in the right circles, rub elbows but never lose yourself. The keyword is sensitivity.

# FEBRUARY WEEK FOUR
# - 22 THRU 28

**2 / 22 / 2023 = 31 / 4**

This day says that obsessiveness, structure, but inactivity shows the duality of the energies. Chaos could be around any corner, look out for it. The keyword is order.

**2 / 23 / 2023 = 14 / 5**

This day says that freedom, imagination, and moderation are the most prominent energies that abound. You may find yourself stubborn which will bring chaos, so avoid that. The keyword is change.

**2 / 24 / 2023 = 15 / 6**

This day says that responsibility, commitment, and love are what is leading the energy charge. Pay attention to being excessive or restless both are lower vibes. The keyword is service to others.

**2 / 25 / 2023 = 16 / 7**

This day says that trusting self, gaining knowledge, and spirituality are the energies to embrace. Avoid over-commitment and infatuation. The keyword is faith.

**2 / 26 / 2023 = 17 / 8**

This day says that finances, material things, and authority are all going to be looking for attention. Being cynical or sarcastic will not help. The keyword is money.

**2 / 27 / 2023 = 18 / 9**

This day says that wisdom, charity, and compassion will all be in the mix energy-wise. Take note of who is in charge for future reference. The keyword is impulse.

**2 / 28 / 2023 = 19 / 10 / 1**

This day says that you should spin the wheel and take a chance, you have a full spectrum before you, see what comes up. Beginnings and endings are at play but remember you cannot have one without the other. The keyword is forward vision.

# 2023 MARCH

This is a 3 month which says that we will be focusing on expression, both verbal and creative, sensitivity, and any sort of communication. With the influence of the 1 year, it will be a good time to make your point, stand firm, and express YOUR opinions. You may be socializing more, gathering friends, and interacting with others. At times you may feel blocked, scattered, or reserved, take some action, or do something to re-invigorate, this is a sign your energy is getting low.

# MARCH WEEK ONE - 1 THRU 7

**3 / 1 / 2023 = MASTER NUMBER 11**

This day says that the Master Teacher is in the building. Your words will have an impact on others today. There are new beginnings coming so be on the lookout. The keyword is stand on your own.

**3 / 2 / 2023 = 12 / 3**

This day says that communication, expression, and sensitivity will be present in many shades. Avoid being caught off guard because it will set you back. Maintain your personal center and you will be fine. The keyword is balance.

3 / 3 / 2023 = 13 / 4

This day says that organization, structure, and work are the energies that will present looking for attention. See the practical matters first. The keyword is action.

**3 / 4 / 2023 = 14 / 5**

This day says that restlessness, random change, and irritability seem to be on energy-wise. Pull your feelings back to the practical. These are subconscious vibrations, they will be felt more than anything else. The keyword is organization.

## 3 / 5 / 2023 = 15 / 6

This day says that love, service to others, and responsibility will be at the forefront asking for commitment. Be careful with those long-term commitments, remember, you get restless. The keyword is adventure.

## 3 / 6 / 2023/ = 16 / 7

This day says that faith, knowl edge, and trust are leading the energy charge, you may be asked to define your spirituality. Knowing your truth and trusting your insight will affect your answer. The keyword is responsibility.

## 3 / 7 / 2023 = 17 / 8

This day says that management of resources, a show of authority, and financial issues will draw your attention. With a need to assert your authority by using the resources at your disposal. You may even hold off any monetary difficulty with your management skills. The keyword is knowledge.

# MARCH WEEK TWO - 8 THRU 14

**3 / 8 / 2023 = 18 / 9**

This day says that you may feel dynamic, impulsive, or generous. Try to avoid selfishness., and judgment as they are the lower vibes. The keyword is karma.

**3 / 9 / 2023 = 19 / 10 / 1**

This day says that independence, inventiveness, and ideals are the energies drawing attention. Seek closure for things not serving any longer and make an aggressive start to any new venture. The keyword is dynamics.

**3 / 10 / 2023 = MASTER NUMBER 11**

This day says that the Master Teacher energy is present, people will heed your words and seek your advice as a knowledgeable individual. The keyword is tact.

**3 / 11 / 2023 = 21 / 3**

This day says that popularity, social interaction, and expression are gearing up to be important. Avoid being either superficial or reserved try to find the middle ground. The keyword is advisor.

**3 / 12 / 2023 = 13 / 4**

This day says that obsessive, structured, and practical are the energies most prominent. Chaos or inactivity may try for a foothold, you need to be aware. The keyword is expression.

**3 / 13 / 2023 = 14 / 5**

This day says that imagination, adventure, and change will be in the mix of energies. See things as you want them to be. Do not avoid things that are different, try them. The keyword is practical.

**3 / 14 / 2023 = 15 / 6**

This day says that commitment, tenacity, and hard-headedness are on the table energy-wise. It is better to do than not to do, and avoid giving the impression of not caring when that is not the case. The keyword is freedom.

# MARCH WEEK THREE
# - 15 THRU 21

**3 / 15 / 2023 = 16 /7**

This day says that introspection, knowledge, and spirituality will be important for you. Gather all the facts before committing, trust but verify. The keyword is love.

**3 / 16 / 2023 = 17 / 8**

This day says that power, authority, and money are the things seeking attention. grasp the power offered, show the well thought-out authority and more money will be forthcoming. The keyword is trust.

**3 / 17 / 2023 = 18 / 9**

This day says that compassion, generosity, and innate wisdom are the energies that will be present. Beware of jealousy or revenge vying for attention, those are lower vibes, raise them to a higher level. The keyword is power.

**3 / 18 / 2023 = 19 / 10 / 1**

This day says that forward vision, inpatients, and sometimes ego are at the forefront energy-wise. Do not allow insecurity to sneak in. The keyword is impulsive.

**3 / 19 / 2023 = 20 / 2**

This day says that balance. tact, and nurturing are the energies most at play. Be careful not to be shy or victimized  today. Just maintain that balance. The keyword is ideals.

**3 / 20 / 2023 = 12 /3**

This day says that sensitivity, creativity, and self-expression are energies that help to show the real you to the world. Know that spirit has your back and being balanced will enhance everything else. The keyword is nurturing.

**3 / 21 / 2023 = 13 / 4**

This day says that stability, organization, and practicality will be the energies seen. Feeling reserved or scattered may sidetrack you for a time. But remember that you have the tools to do this. The keyword is creativity.

# MARCH WEEK FOUR - 22 THRU 28

**3 / 22 / 2023 = 32 / 5**

This day says that physical activity, personal freedom, and random change are all in the forcast. Let the sensitive caring you go first, to keep all those other traits in line. The keyword is motherhood or parenthood.

**3 / 23 / 2023 = 15 / 6**

This day says that responsibility, love, and service to others are the energies you will experience. Shake off that restless feeling and move forward with purpose. The keyword is imagination.

**3 / 24 / 2023 = 16 / 7**

This day says that introspection, knowledge, and trusting self are what is needing to be addressed. Look within and love what you see. The keyword is self appreciation.

**3 / 25 / 2023 = 17 / 8**

This day says that karma, spiritual vs. material, and power are the energies working here. Put aside sarcasm, and cynicism, they do not serve. If you see karma, dispel it (see afterword) for good. The keyword is trust.

## 3 / 26 / 2023 = 18 / 9

This day says that ancient wisdom, altruism, and impulses will be the energies seen. We carry wisdom from long ago and use it on a daily basis, it helps curb our impulses and puts the give back in giving. The keyword is money.

## 3 / 27 / 2023 = 19 / 10 / 1

This day says that new beginnings, fresh starts, and taking a chance will all be present energy-wise. See what works for you from the entire spectrum presented. Seek a compassionate match. The keyword is wisdom.

## 3 / 28 / 2023 = 20 / 2

This day says that persuasion, emotion, and indecision are all present and will be felt. Use the tools you have and do not let emotion rule. Find your personal center and decide from a place of balance. The keyword is independence.

# MARCH WEEK FIVE - 29 THRU 31

**3 / 29 / 2023 = 21 / 3**

This day says that communication, creativity, and expression are looking for attention. Speak your truth in whatever unique way you have of expressing yourself. The keyword is to teach.

**3 / 30 / 2023 = 13 / 4**

This day says that work, stability, and structure are the energies at play. You see the transition happening, embrace it, things may just be enhanced by it. The keyword is communication.

**3 / 31 / 2023 = 14 / 5**

This day says that imagination, adventure, and moderation will be in the mix of energies. Be excited to see what is coming and exercise moderation in all activities. The keyword is structure.

# 2023 APRIL

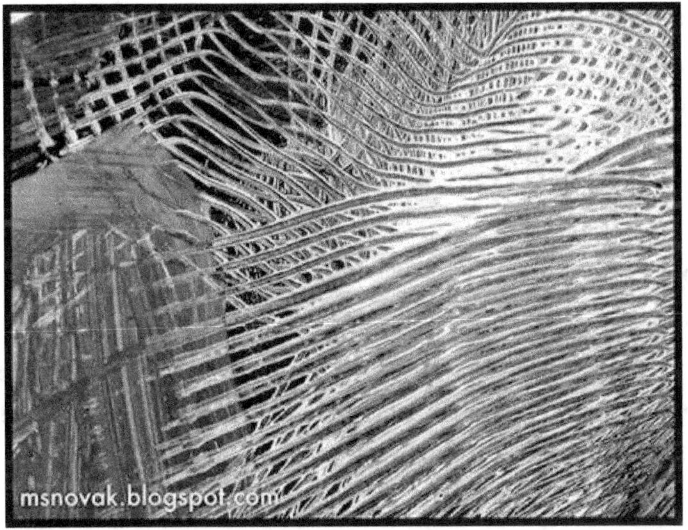


This is a 4 month which says there will be much attention to work, structure, organization,  and stability this month. It is a time to take care of practical matters that may have been put off lately. You have built on a solid foundation, do not let forgetfulness or neglect crumble that foundation, take care of it now. There will be the desire to just blow it off,  but you need to focus, not be stubborn or obsessive. Show everyone your true colors and organize that chaos

# APRIL WEEK ONE – 1 THRU 7

**4 / 1 / 2023 = 12 / 3**

This day says that popularity, social interaction, and sensitivity may be on the table. Reservation and feeling scattered can derail any social activity. The keyword is inviting.

**4 / 2 / 2023 = 13 / 4**

This day says that organization, work, and structure are important energy-wise. Chaos is not practical and will destabilize you. The keyword is partnership.

**4 / 3 / 2023 = 14 / 5**

This day says that change, physical activity, and excesses are the energies you will see. Being restrained makes you irritable, so practice moderation. The keyword is action.

**4 / 4 / 2023 = 15 / 6**

This day says that commitment, service, and responsability will be in the mix energy-wise. Obstinance is sometimes seen as uncaring, or noncommittal and is lower vibes. The keyword is stubborn.

**4 / 5 / 2023 = 16 / 7**

This day says that being well informed, having faith, and trusting can be of importance. Avoid isolation and being skeptical. The keyword is restless.

**4 / 6 / 2023 = 17 / 8**

This day says that management, administrative skills, and authority are the energies to look for.  Save analysis and cynicism for another day. The keyword is commitment.

**4 / 7 / 2023 = 18 / 9**

This day says that charity, dynamics, and compassion will present themselves for attention. Do not judge or be resentful, both are lower vibes and should be avoided. The keyword is spirituality.

# APRIL WEEK TWO - 8 THRU 14

**4 / 8 / 2023 = 19 / 10 / 1**

This day says that independence, ideals, and inventiveness. will stand up and be heard. The forceful visionary or the strong ego will also be present. The keyword is power.

**4 / 9 / 2023 = 20 / 2**

This day says that balance, nurturing, and tact are on call energy-wise. Keep your eyes open for deceit in any form. The keyword is dynamics.

**4 / 10 / 2023 = 12 / 3**

This day says that creativity, expression, and sensitivity are in the mix of energy we will see. Create what you want and stay centered. The keyword is ideals.

**4 / 11 / 2023 = MASTER NUMBER 22**

This day says that the Master potential is present in spades, both in the total and the date. Speak clearly and lay a strong foundation, all is possible. The keyword is mentor.

**4 / 12 / 2023 = 14 / 5**

This day says that freedom, restlessness, and irritability are the energies looking for attention. Avoid restraint but be adventurous. The keyword is create.

**4 / 13 / 2023 = 15 / 6**

This day says that love, determination, and control are at the forefront of leading the energy train. Tame chaos when it crops up. The keyword is transition.

**4 / 14 / 2023 = 16 / 7**

This day says that spiritual, analytical, and skeptical are the potpourri of energies available. Such a dichotomy, avoid being cynical or isolated. The keyword is freedom.

# APRIL WEEK THREE - 15 THRU 21

**4 / 15 / 2023 = 17 / 8**

This day says that material things, money, and power will show themselves. Be aware any one energy can take focus from the others. The keyword is love.

**4 / 16 / 2023 = 18 / 9**

This day says that compassion, altruism, and impulse are the energies at work here. Be sure not to fall into the "what's in it for me" trap, that is a whole other discussion. The keyword is motivation.

**4 / 17 / 2023 = 19 / 10 / 1**

This day says that it may be time to be forceful, share your vision and welcome innovation. Put the modest insecure you on the shelf and declare yourself. The keyword is authority.

**4 / 18 / 2023 = 20 / 2**

This day says that you are persuasive, centered, and sometimes too emotional and those are the energies you will be seeing, Watch for deception, and DO NOT allow yourself to be a victim. The keyword is closure.

**4 / 19 / 2023 = 21 / 3**

This day says that communication, self-expression, and action are the energies at play. Not feeling yourself or feeling blocked may try to keep you down. Rally and be that DO-ER that everybody loves. The keyword is DO IT!

**4 / 20 / 2023 = 13 / 4**

This day says that practical, organized, and structured are the prominent energies at work. Curb your sometimes obsessive nature and avoid chaos. The keyword is balance.

**4 / 21 / 2023 = 14 / 5**

This day says that random change, physical activity, and moderation will all be present energy-wise. Avoid excesses, restraint, or restlessness. The keyword is communicate.

# APRIL WEEK FOUR - 22 THRU 28

**4 / 22 / 2023 = MASTER NUMBER 33**

This day says that Master potential abounds with the Master Communicator and the Master Teacher. Say what you feel, and others will feel it. Whatever you put out send it with love and warmth. The keyword is order

**4 / 23 / 2023 = 16 / 7**

This day says that introspection, knowledge, and faith will be important factors to consider. Sarcasm and building walls are defense tactics and do little to raise your vibrations. The keyword is change.

**4 / 24 / 2023 = 17 / 8**

This day says that administrative skills, management of resources, and material vs. spiritual are the energies present and looking for attention. Avoid jealousy because you have everything you need. The keyword is responsibility.

**4 / 25 / 2023 = 18 / 9**

This day says that ancient innate wisdom, charity and compassion are on tap energy-wise We all carry ancient wisdom and use it on a daily basis. The keyword is knowledge.

**4 / 26 / 2023 = 19 / 10 / 1**

This day says that new starts, bold ventures, and fresh enterprises will all be available energy-wise, take advantage. The seeds previously sown are showing themselves. The keyword is material things.

**4 / 27 / 2023 = 20 / 2**

This day says that emotion, indecision, and thoughtless words may show up. Try re-centering yourself, see a mirror before you that reflects your words back to you so you can feel their impact. The keyword is impulsive.

**4 / 28 / 2023 = 21 / 3**

This day says that action, communication, and social situations will be the most prominent. Feeling blocked, scattered, or just generally reserved may also need attention. The keyword is brilliant ideas.

# APRIL WEEK FIVE -
# 29 THRU 30

**4 / 29 / 2023 = MASTER NUMBER 22**

This day says that the Master Builder in you can bring order to chaotic situations. Use this potential while it is present. Avoid being shy or having emotional outbursts. The keyword is persuasive.

**4 / 30 / 2023 = 14 / 5**

This day says that restraint, excesses, and change are the energies at play here. Exercise your freedom, and practice moderation, there is nothing to do about the changes except deal with them. The keyword is creativity.

# 2023 MAY

This is a 5 month that says changes are in the wind, moderation will need to be practiced. Your imagination is going to work overtime, and you will be experiencing a need to be unencumbered. Not a major fan of change? Join the club, but you are going to have to accept it. Take a look at things you may have done to excess in the recent past and use restraint this time. Try harnessing those brilliant ideas and act on them, before you get restless and bored.

# MAY WEEK ONE - 1 THRU 7

**5 / 1 / 2023 = 13 / 4**

This day says that work, chaos, and obsessions will be present. There is a stubborn streak seen also, try regaining some order. The keyword is innovation

**5 / 2 / 2023 = 14 / 5**

This day says that freedom, physical activity, and moderation will rule the energies. Restraint and feeling jumpy may haunt you, center yourself and go on. The keyword is level.

**5 / 3 / 2023 = 15 / 6**

This day says that responsibility, commitment, and service to others are the energies present. Take commitment seriously and try not to appear uncaring or irresponsible. The keyword is self-expression.

**5 / 4 / 2023 = 16 / 7**

This day says that trust, spirituality, and faith are strong energies showing their presents here. Stay connected to those that matter and avoid isolating yourself. The keyword is structure.

**5 / 5 / 2023 = 17 / 8**

This day says that power, authority, and management skills are the energies prominent here. Watch your finances or feeling jealous, because they are energetically  connected. The keyword is restless.

**5 / 6 / 2023 = 18 / 9**

This day says that you may feel dynamic, impulsive, or generous. Try to avoid selfishness., and judgment as they are the lower vibes. The keyword is love.

**5 / 7 / 2023 = 19 / 10 / 1**

This day says that independence, innovation, and ideals will be the energies at play here. No room for modesty or insecurity, stand on your own and rule the day. The keyword is introspection.

# MAY WEEK TWO - 8 THRU 14

**5 / 8 / 2023 = 20 / 2**

This day says that persuasion, tact, and balance are all involved here. Be sure not to be shy or indecisive when interacting with others. The keyword is management.

**5 / 9 / 2023 = 21 / 3**

This day says that communication, feelings, and self-expression are all paramount. Maintaining your balance and staying centered will help. The keyword is compassion.

**5 / 10 / 2023 = 13 / 4**

This day says that work, organization, structure, and stability are what will present looking for attention. See what needs doing and do it, no discussion is necessary. The keyword is independence.

**5 / 11 / 2023 = 23 / 5**

This day says that adventure, change, and excess are the most prominent energies at work. Explore, expect changes, and do not overdo it. The keyword is advise.

**5 / 12 / 2023 = 15 / 6**

This day says that love, service to others, and responsibility will be at the forefront asking for commitment. Be careful with those long terms, remember, you get restless. The keyword is expression.

**5 / 13 / 2023 = 16 / 7**

This day says that faith, knowledge, and trust are leading the energy charge, you may be asked to define your spirituality. Knowing your truth and trusting your insight will have a bearing on the answer you give, The keyword is stability.

**5 / 14 / 2023 = 17 / 8**

This day says that authority, management, and power will be in the mix. You may be asked to trust but do not do that blindly, always verify. The keyword is imagination.

# MAY WEEK THREE
# - 15 THRU 21

**5 / 15 / 2023 = 18 / 9**

This day says that wisdom, charity, and compassion will all be in the mix energy-wise. Take note of who is in charge for future reference. The keyword is commitment.

**5 / 16 / 2023 = 19 / 10 / 1**

This day says that innovation, industrious deeds, and an inventive mindset all are at the mark, waiting for the signal to go. New beginnings are coming so make the best of them. The keyword is faith

**5 / 17 / 2023 = 20 / 2**

This day says that balance, tact, and nurturing are the energies most at play. Be careful not to be shy or victimized. Just maintain that balance. The keyword is power.

**5 / 18 / 2023 = 21 /3**

This day says that creativity, expression, and sensitivity will be the energies present. Social interaction is important, along with communication. The keyword is wisdom

## 5 / 19 / 2023 = MASTER NUMBER 22

This day says that the Master Builder potential is present and raising the normal vibrations to a higher level. use it to put things in order and tame the chaos. The keyword is visionary.

## 5 / 20 / 2023 = 14 / 5

This day says that imagination, adventure, and change will be in the mix of energies. See things as you want them to be. Do not avoid things that are different, try them. The keyword is tact.

## 5 / 21 / 2023 = 15 / 6

This day says that infatuation, responsibility, and tenacity are presenting themselves. Avoid being restless, excessive, and moody. The keyword is creativity

# MAY WEEK FOUR - 22 THRU 28

**5 / 22 / 2023 = 34 / 7**

This day says that analytics, sarcasm, and being cynical are energies you may see or feel. These are all lower vibes,  which means your personal vibration is too low, try to raise it and center yourself. The keyword is foundation.

**5 / 23 / 2023 = 17 / 8**

This day says that money, power, and management are the focus. Managing time, money and people will go a long way toward establishing your power. Be careful whom you trust. The keyword is freedom.

**5 / 24 / 2023 = 18 / 9**

This day says that imagination, physical effort, and excesses are the prominent energies. Do not show your stubborn side and avoid chaos. The keyword is commitment.

**5 / 25 / 2023 = 19 / 10 / 1**

This day says that independence, standing on your own, and speaking your truth will be important. Keep your eyes open for that new beginning or a fresh start and maintain your balance.The keyword is trust.

**5 / 26 / 2023 = 20 / 2**

This day says that balance. tact, and nurturing are the energies most at play. Be careful not to be shy or victimized today. Just maintain that balance. The keyword is power.

**5 / 27 / 2023 = 21 / 3**

This day says that sensitivity, creativity, and self-expression are energies that help to show the real you to the world. Know that spirit has your back and being balanced will enhance everything else. The keyword is compassion.

**5 / 28 / 2023 = MASTER NUMBER 22**

This day says that the Master potential is present in the Master Builder bringing energies that will influence the many instead of the few. The keyword is innovation.

# MAY WEEK FIVE - 29 THRU 31

**5 / 29 / 2023 = 23 / 5**

This day says that imagination, adventure, and moderation will be in the mix of energies. Be excited to see what is coming and exercise moderation in all activities. The keyword is mentor.

**5 / 30 / 2023 = 15 / 6**

This day says that responsibility, love, and service to others are the energies you will experience. Shake off that restless feeling and move forward with purpose. The keyword is sensitivity.

**5 / 31 / 2023 = 16 / 7**

This day says that being well informed, having faith, and trusting can be of importance. Avoid being skeptical and being alone. The keyword is organization.

# 2023 JUNE

This is a 6 month which says that is all about love, commitment, responsibility, and the support of others. Take responsibility for your actions and words, commit with your whole heart, and love loudly. The influence of the month will make all of these actions very personal. Try to avoid letting your ego dictate your actions, that will make you seem uncaring and obstinate.

# JUNE WEEK ONE - 1 THRU 7

**6 / 1 / 2023 = 14 / 5**

This day says that change, physical activity, and excesses are the energies you will see. Being restrained makes you irritable because you value your freedom. The keyword is independence.

**6 / 2 / 2023 = 15 / 6**

This day says that commitment, service, and responsibility will be in the mix energy-wise. Obstinance is seen as uncaring, or noncommittal avoid this lower vibe. The keyword is balanced.

**6 / 3 / 2023 = 16 / 7**

This day says that introspection, knowledge, and trusting self are what is needing to be addressed. Look within and trust what you see, do not be derailed by love. The keyword is sensitivity.

**6 / 4 / 2023 = 17 / 8**

This day says that karma, material things, and power are the energies working here. Put aside sarcasm, and cynicism, they do not serve. If you feel a karmic tie, dispel it (see afterword) for good. The keyword is work.

**6 / 5 / 2023 = 18 / 9**

This day says that compassion, altruism, and impulse are the energies at work here. If you ask "what's in it for me" you missed the boat on altruism altogether. The keyword is change.

**6 / 6 / 2023 = 19 / 10 / 1**

This day says that independence, ideals, and inventiveness will stand up and be heard. The impulsive visionary or the strong ego will also be present. The keyword is service to others.

**6 / 7 / 2023 = 20 / 2**

This day says that balance, nurturing, and tact are on call energy-wise. Keep your eyes open for lies or betrayals, in any form, and be aware. The keyword is trust but verify.

# JUNE WEEK TWO - 8 THRU 14

**6 / 8 / 2023 = 21 / 3**

This day says that sensitivity, creativity, and self-expression are energies that help to show the real you to the world. Maintain your balance and independence. The keyword is authority.

**6 / 9 / 2023 = MASTER NUMER 22**

This day says that the Master potential is present in the form of the Master Builder, time to bring order to the chaos. Lay a solid foundation, and sever ties that no longer serve you. The keyword is endings.

**6 / 10 / 2023 = 14 / 5**

This day says that physical activity, personal freedom, and random change are all on board. Let the sensible caring you go first, to keep all those other errant traits in line. The keyword is forceful.

**6 / 11 / 2023 = 24 / 6**

This day says that responsibility, love, and service to others are the energies you will see. Commit your effort to balance and stability. The keyword is leading the way.

**6 / 12 / 2023 = 16 / 7**

This day says that being well informed, having faith, and trusting will be of importance. Avoid listening to others before you listen to your own heart. The keyword is sensitivity.

**6 / 13 / 2023 = 17 / 8**

This day says that management, administrative skills, and authority are in play. This may be a time to delegate power elsewhere. The keyword is structure.

**6 / 14 / 2023 = 18 / 9**

This day says that ancient wisdom, altruism, and impulses will be the energies seen. We carry wisdom and use it daily, it helps curb our impulses. The keyword is activity.

# JUNE WEEK THREE
# - 15 THRU 21

**6 / 15 / 2023 = 19 / 10 / 1**

This day says that independence, ideals, and innovation will stand up and be heard. Beware a powerful ego or the compassionate impulsive soul that may also be present. The keyword is responsibility.

**6 / 16 / 2023 = 20 / 2**

This day says that persuasion, emotion, and insecurity are all present and will be felt. Use the tools you have and do not let lower vibes rule. Seek your personal center and ban insecure feelings from you. The keyword is trust.

**6 / 17 / 2023 = 21 / 3**

This day says that creativity, expression, and sensitivity are in the mix of energy we will see. Create what you want and stay in balance. The keyword is management.

**6 / 18 / 2023 = MASTER NUMBER 22**

This day says that the potential is present in the Master Builder bringing energies that will influence the many instead of the few.

This number speaks to a strong need for balance. The keyword is compassion.

**6 / 19 / 2023 = 23 / 5**

This day says that adventure, change, and excess are the most prominent energies. Explore, expect changes, and avoid overdoing things. The keyword is a fresh start.

**6 / 20 / 2023 = 15 / 6**

This day says that service to others, commitment, and responsibility will be in the mix energy-wise. Look out for that obstinate streak, it is sometimes a subconscious vibration and should be avoided. The keyword is nurturing.

**6 / 21 / 2023 = 16 / 7**

This day says that spiritual, analytical, and skeptical are the dichotomy of energies available. Such a potpourri, avoid isolation and being cynical. The keyword is expression.

# JUNE WEEK FOUR - 22 THRU 28

**6 / 22 / 2023 = 35 / 8**

This day says that administrative skills, management, and material concerns are the energies present and looking for attention. Guard against feelings of revenge or worry about money. The keyword is organization.

**6 / 23 / 2023 = 18 / 9**

This day says that charity, altruism, compassion, and foresight are the energies at work here. Watch out for the subconscious vibrations of insecurity, jealousy, or revenge. The keyword is adventure

**6 / 24 / 2023 = 19 / 10 / 1**

This day says that it may be time to share your foresight,  and vision and welcome innovation. Put the modest insecure you away and declare yourself. The keyword is responsibility.

**6 / 25 / 2023 = 20 / 2**

This day says that balance, nurturing, and tact are on call energy-wise. Watch out for emotional betrayal or deceit in any form. The keyword is faith.

## 6 / 26 / 2023 = 21 / 3

This day says that popularity, social interaction, and expression may be on the table. Feeling blocked or scattered may crop up to derail your positive social efforts. The keyword is authority.

## 6 / 27 / 2023 =MASTER NUMBER 22

This day says that the Master Builder in you can bring order to any chaotic situation. Use this potential while it is present. Avoid being emotional or becoming a victim. The keyword is charity.

## 6 / 28 / 2023 = 23 / 5

This day says that change, physical activity, and excesses are the energies you will see. Being restless and irritable will also be seen but are lower vibes, so practice moderation. The keyword is getting a fresh start.

# JUNE WEEK FIVE - 29 THRU 30

**6 / 29 / 2023 = 24 / 6**

This day says that commitment, love, and service to others are the energies present. Take commitment seriously, and try not to entertain lower vibes like uncaring or irresponsibility. The keyword is influence.

**6 / 30 / 2023 = 16 / 7**

This day says that trust, faith, and spirituality are strong energies showing their presents. Stay connected to those people in your life who matter, and avoid isolation. The keyword is expression.

# 2023 JULY

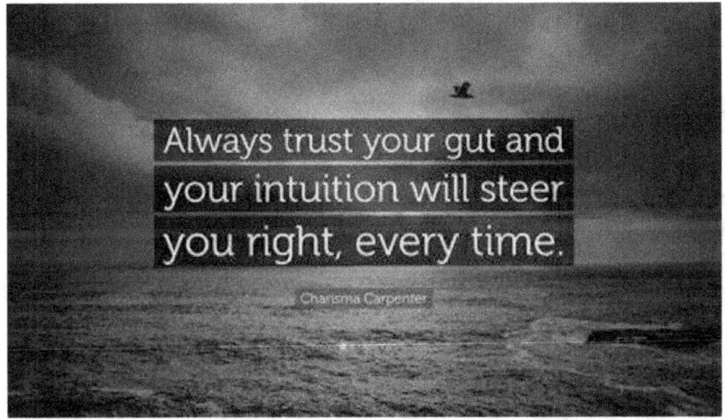


This is a 7 month, and it mirrors the vibration of the year bringing introspection, knowledge, and trust by the boatload this month. It is important to learn the value of communication with your higher self. There is schooling somewhere in the cards for you if you chose,  and opportunities to place your trust in someone or something with which you have no track record. Some would call it an act of blind faith, but I say trust your gut and you will know what to do.

# JULY WEEK ONE - I THRU 7

**7 / 1 / 2023 = 15 / 6**

This day says that love, control, and responsibility are at the front of the energy train. Tenacity and obstinance may crop up as subconscious feelings. The keyword is independence.

**7 / 2 / 2023 = 16 / 7**

This day says that trust, spirituality, and introspection are energies showing their presents. Stay in the moment, avoid cynicism and isolating yourself. The keyword is nurturing.

**7 / 3 / 2023 = 17 / 8**

This day says that management skills, power, and authority, are the prominent energies. Watch your finances or feelings of revenge because they are energetically connected. The keyword is creativity.

**7 / 4 / 2023 = 18 / 9**

This day says that compassion, wisdom, and charity are the energies here. What will,be important is independence and power. The keyword is stability.

**7 / 5 / 2023 = 19 / 10 / 1f**

This day says that innovation, inventiveness, and ideals are in the works. It could be time to welcome changes as needed. Show your vision and assertiviness to all. The keyword is freedom.

**7 / 6 / 2023 = 20 / 2**

This day says that you are persuasive, centered, and sometimes too emotional you will be seeing those energies. Watch for any falsehood or deception. The keyword is responsible.

**7 / 7 / 2023 = 21 / 3**

This day says that self-expression, sensitivity, and taking action are the energies at play. Much activity in the cosmos may have you feeling out of sorts or blocked. The keyword is faith.

# JULY WEEK TWO - 8 THRU 14

**7 / 8 / 2023 = MASTER NUMBER 22**

This day says that the Master Builder can bring order to chaotic situations. Use this potential while it is present and pull from this Master energy to accomplish your goals. The keyword is manifest.

**7 / 9 / 2023 = 23 / 5**

This day says that random change, physical activity, and moderation will all be present energy-wise. Feeling out of sorts or overly sensitive will keep you off balance. The keyword is compassion.

**7 / 10 / 2023 = 15 / 6**

This day says that responsibility, commitment, and service to others are the energies present. Own your actions and commitment seriously and try not to appear uncaring or irresponsible. The keyword is stand on your own.

**7 / 11 / 2023 = 25 / 7**

This day says that spirituality, faith, and trust are strong energies showing here. Stay centred and take care not to be excessive. The keyword is teaching others.

**7 / 12 / 2023 = 17 / 8**

This day says that administrative skills, management, and money are the energies present and looking for attention. Trust your inner voice and guard your independence. The keyword is communication.

**7 / 13 / 2023 = 18 / 9**

This day says that ancient innate wisdom, compassion, and charity are on tap energy-wise. Carrying ancient wisdom and being able to tap into it is special, know that. The keyword is organization.

**7 / 14 / 2023 = 19 / 10 / 1**

This day says that fresh starts, exciting ventures, and new enterprises will all be available energy-wise. Take advantage of the seeds previously sown. Do not stand at a closed door waiting for it to reopen. The keyword is change.

# JULY WEEK THREE
# – 15 THRU 21

**7 / 15 / 2023 = 20 / 2**

This day says that thoughtless words and emotion may show up. Try seeing a mirror before you that reflects your words so you can feel their impact. The keyword is caring.

**7 / 16 / 2023 = 21 / 3**

This day says that action and communication will be the most prominent. Having your thoughts scattered is a lower vibe, re-center, and move forward. The keyword is introspection.

**7 / 17 / 2023 = MASTER NUMBER 22**

This day says that the Master Builder is present, who can stabilize sagging foundations. Use this potential while it is present. Avoid having emotional outbursts or being indecisive. The keyword is finance.

**7 / 18 / 2023 = 23 / 5**

This day says that freedom, change, and excesses are the energies looking for attention. Avoid restraint but be adventurous. The keyword is generosity.

**7 / 19 / 2023 = 24 / 6**

This day says that work, order, and obsessions will be present, working against one another. Try looking at your emotions and organizing things better. The keyword is a new venture.

**7 / 20 / 2023 = 16 / 7**

This day says that faith, trust, and spirituality are strong energies here. Stay connected to those who matter, and avoid idle commitment. The keyword is centered.

**7 / 21 / 2023 = 17 / 8**

This day says that power, authority, and management skills are the energies prominent here. Watch cynical feelings or your lack of faith in certain things because they are connected. The keyword is sensitivity.

# JULY WEEK FOUR – 22 THRU 28

**7 / 22 / 2023 = 36 / 9**

This day says that charity, wisdom, and compassion are the energy present. Communication and commitment  may be scattered or adversely affected. The keyword is structure.

**7 / 23 / 2023 = 19 / 10 / 1**

This day says that independence, innovation, and ideals will be the energies here. No room for modesty or impulsive actions, stand on your own feet and rule the day. The keyword is imagination.

**7 / 24 / 2023 = 20 / 2**

This day says that emotion, balance, and nurturing will have a big energetic impact. Avoid indecision and being deceptive. The keyword is service to others.

**7 / 25 / 2023 = 21 / 3**

This day says that communication, social situations, and action will be the most prominent. Feeling blocked, scattered, or just generally reserved may also need attention. The keyword is spirituality.

**7 / 26 / 2023 = MASTER NUMBER 22**

This day says that this Master Number is bringing Master energy potential to play here. The Master Builder is structured, stable, and able to tame the most chaotic situation. The keyword is management.

**7 / 27 / 2023 = 23 / 5**

This day says that physical activity, freedom, and moderation will rule the energies. Indecisive and feeling scattered and may haunt you, center yourself and go on. The keyword is wisdom

**7 / 28 / 2023 = 24 / 6**

This day says that responsibility, commitment, and service are the energies present. Commit wholeheartedly and be of service willingly. The keyword is independence.

# JULY WEEK FIVE - 29 THRU 31

**7 / 29 / 2023 = 25 / 7**

This day says that trust, spirituality, and faith are strong energies showing their presents. Keep your connections strong, try not to get irritated. The keyword is mentor.

**7 / 30 / 2023 = 17 / 8**

This day says that authority, power, and management skills are the energies prominent here. Watch your money or feeling jealous because they are connected energetically. The keyword is communication.

**7 / 31 / 2023 = 18 / 9**

This day says that you may feel dynamic, impulsive, or generous. Avoid judgment or selfishness, as they are the lower vibrations. The keyword is stability.

# 2023 AUGUST

This is an 8 month and is all about power, authority, and material things. You can show your knack for the management of time, people, and money. There is a delicate balance between the spiritual and the material with this number. Be aware of which realm you are working in because the resources are sometimes different. Change is also a strong possibility because you have thought about it, weighed the pros and cons, and are now ready to execute a well-thought-out plan.

# AUGUST WEEK ONE - 1 THRU 7

**8 / 1 / 2023 = 16 / 7**

This day says that spirituality, faith, and trust, are energies showing here. Stay committed and maintain your individuality. The keyword is innovation.

**8 / 2 / 2023 = 17 / 8**

This day says that management, authority, and power are the energies prominent here. Look within to discover what you are missing. The keyword is partnership.

**8 / 3 / 2023 = 18 / 9**

This day says that you may feel dynamic, impulsive, or generous. Be careful with your money and know that revenge is counterproductive, and has a lower vibration. The keyword is expression.

**8 / 4 / 2023 = 19 / 10 / 1**

This day says that inventiveness, innovation, and ideals will be the energies at work here. No room for modesty or insecurity, use your ancient wisdom and rule the day. The keyword is organization.

**8 / 5 / 2023 = 20 / 2**

This day says that balance, tact, and nurturing are the energies most at play. Be careful not to be too emotional it could lead to being victimized. Just maintain your balance. The keyword is change.

**8 / 6 / 2023 = 21 / 3**

This day says that creativity, expression, and sensitivity will be the energies present. Communication especially in social situations may be challenging. The keyword is response to others.

**8 / 7 / 2023 = MASTER NUMBER 22**

This day says that the Master Builder potential is present and raising the normal vibrations to a higher level. Use it to put things in order and tame the chaos. powerful energies abound. The keyword is look within.

# AUGUST WEEK TWO
# - 8 THRU 14

**8 / 8 / 2023 = 23 / 5**

This day says that adventure, change, and excess are the most prominent energies at work. Explore, expect changes, try not to overdo it, and enjoy the new adventure. The keyword is finances.

**8 / 9 / 2023 = 24 / 6**

This day says that love, service to others, and responsibility will be at the forefront asking for commitment. Be aware of the structure of things before you commit. The keyword is charity.

**8 / 10 / 2023 = 16 / 7**

This day says that introspection, trusting self, and knowledge is what is needing to be addressed. Look within and trust what you see, do not be derailed by love. The keyword is self-awareness.

**8 / 11 / 2023 = 26 / 8**

This day says that management, administrative skills, and authority are in play. Too much commitment will take a toll so you may want to delegate power to others. The keyword is lead the way.

**8 / 12 / 2023 = 18 / 9**

This day says that compassion, altruism, and impulse are the energies at work here. If you ask "what's in it for me" you missed the boat on altruism altogether. The keyword is action

**8 / 13 / 2023 = 19 / 10 / 1**

This day says that independence, ideals, and innovation will stand up and be heard. Control your ego but also watch for the compassionate impulsive soul that may also be present. The keyword is work.

**8 / 14 / 2023 = 20 / 2**

This day says that tact, balance, and nurturing are on call energy-wise. Look out for lies or betrayals, in any form. Keep your emotions under control. The keyword is activity.

# AUGUST WEEK THREE
# - 15 THRU 21

**8 / 15 / 2023 = 21 / 3**

This day says that sensitivity, creativity, and self-expression are the energies that show the real you. Know that being balanced and independent will enhance everything else. The keyword is love.

**8 / 16 / 2023 = MASTER NUMBER 22**

This day says that the Master Builder potential is present bringing energies that will influence the many instead of the few. You may need to continually balance and re-center yourself. The keyword is knowledge.

**8 / 17 / 2023 = 23 / 5**

This day says that imagination, adventure, and moderation will be present. Be excited to see what is coming but avoid excesses in your activities. The keyword is power.

**8 / 18 / 2023 = 24 / 6**

This day says that responsibility, love, and service to others are the energies you will see. Maintain your balance and work toward stabilizing your environment. The keyword is charity.

**8 / 19 / 2023 = 25 / 7**

This day says that faith, spirituality, and trust are strong energies here. Avoid excesses and maintain your delicate balance. The keyword is look with fresh eyes.

**8 / 20 / 2023 = 17 / 8**

This day says that material things, power, and karma are the energies working here. Put aside sarcasm, and cynicism, they do not serve. If you feel a karmic tie, dispel it (see afterword) for good. The keyword is balance.

**8 / 21 / 2023 = 18 / 9**

This day says that compassion, altruism, and impulse are the prominent energies here. If you ask "what's in it for me"  you missed the lesson. The keyword is action.

# AUGUST WEEK FOUR
# - 22 THRU 28

**8 / 22 / 2023 = 37 / 10 / 1**

This day says that independence, speaking your truth, and standing up for your ideals will be important. Keep your eyes open for that new enterprise or interesting venture. The keyword is stable ground.

**8 / 23 / 2023 = 20 / 2**

This day says that balance. tact, and nurturing are the energies most at play. Do not play the victim or be shy today. Just maintain your balance. Spirit has your back. The keyword is to physically move forward.

**8 / 24 / 2023 = 21 / 3**

This day says that sensitivity, communication, and self-expression are the energies present and show the real you to the world. Maintain your balance and independence. The keyword is commitment.

**8 / 25 / 2023 = MASTER NUMBER 22**

This day says that the Master potential is present and raising the normal vibrations to a higher level. The Master Builder can put things in order and can tame the most chaotic situations. The keyword is knowledge.

**8 / 26 / 2023 = 23 / 5**

This day says that imagination, adventure, and moderation will be in the mix of energies. Show your enthusiasm about what is coming but exercise moderation in all physical activities. The keyword is management.

**8 / 27 / 2023 = 24 / 6**

This day says that responsibility, love, and service to others are the energies you will see. Focus your efforts on  balance and stability. The keyword is compassion.

**8 / 28 / 2023 = 25 / 7**

This day says that analytics, sarcasm, and being cynical are energies you may see or feel. This means, raise your personal vibration, it is too low. Listen to happy music, walk on the earth, or center yourself. The keyword is get out of your head.

# AUGUST WEEK FIVE - 29 THRU 31

**8 / 29 / 2023 = 26 / 8**

This day says that management, money, and power, are the focus. Managing time, money and people will establish your power. Beware of long term-commitments. The keyword is advisor.

**8 / 30 / 2023 = 18 / 9**

This day says that ancient wisdom, charity, and impulses will be the energies seen. We carry innate wisdom, some say it is the angel that sits on your shoulder, it helps to curb our impulses. The keyword is perception.

**8 / 31 / 2023 = 19 / 10 / 1**

This day says that innovation, industrious deeds, and an inventive mindset all are lining up energy-wise. New beginnings are coming, do not stand at a closed door, look around you. The keyword is work.

# 2023 SEPTEMBER

This is a 9 month, which says that is all about compassion, generosity, and charity, you are being asked to give of yourself without a second thought for yourself, in other words, altruism. Dynamic energies are at play right now, it is just the cosmos showing off its skills. Avoid being impulsive or selfish, those lower vibrations do not serve you. Show your compassion and charity and use your innate ancient wisdom to help fill in any blanks.

# SEPTEMBER WEEK ONE - 1 THRU 7

**9 / 1 / 2023 = 17 / 8**

This day says that material things, power, and karma are the energies working here. Put aside sarcasm, and cynicism. If you feel a karmic pull, dispel it (see afterword) for good. The keyword is fresh new starts.

**9 / 2 / 2023 = 18 / 9**

This day says that innate wisdom, generosity, and compassion are on tap energy-wise We all carry inner power or wisdom and use it to help us be who we are. The keyword is being tactful

**9 / 3 / 2023 = 19 / 10 / 1**

This day says that independence, ideals, and inventiveness will stand up and be heard. The voice of an impulsive visionary or a strong ego will also be present. The keyword is communication.

**9 / 4 / 2023 = 20 / 2**

This day says that emotion, indecision, and thoughtless words may show up. Use an imaginary mirror before you that reflects your words back to you so you can feel their impact. The keyword is practical.

**9 / 5 / 2023 = 21 / 3**

This day says that creativity, expression, and sensitivity will be the energies present. Social interaction and communication will be important. The keyword is physical activity.

**9 / 6 / 2023 = MASTER NUMBER 22**

This day says that the Master potential is present in the form of the Master Builder, time to bring order to the chaos, and lay a solid foundation. Consider building something new and different. The keyword is commitment.

**9 / 7 / 2023 = 23 / 5**

This day says that adventure, change, and excess are the most prominent energies at work. Explore unknown places, don't just think about it do it, and don't be shy. The keyword is trust.

# SEPTEMBER WEEK TWO - 8 THRU 14

**9 / 8 / 2023 = 24 / 6**

This day says that service to others, commitment, and responsibility will be in the mix energy-wise. Look out for that stubborn streak, as long as you maintain your balance you should be fine. The keyword is authority.

**9 / 9 / 2023 = 25 / 7**

This day says that being well informed, having faith, and trusting can be of importance. Look within for your answers. Avoid being indecisive or restless. The keyword is wisdom.

**9 / 10 / 2023 = 17 / 8**

This day says that management, administrative skills, and authority are in play. Handle what you can but look at sharing some authority it may be time to delegate. The keyword is innovation.

**9 / 11 / 2023 = 27 / 9**

This day says that charity, wisdom, and compassion are the energies at work here. Keep an eye out for the lower vibes of shyness or a loss of faith. The keyword is influence.

**9 / 12 / 2023 = 19 / 10 / 1**

This day says that independence, standing on your own, and speaking your truth will be important. Look for that new beginning or a fresh start and maintain your balance. The keyword is creativity.

**9 / 13 / 2023 = 20 / 2**

This day says that nurturing, balance, and tact are the energy seen here. Keep your eyes open for lies or betrayals, spirit will alert you so be aware. The keyword is transformation.

**9 / 14 / 2023 = 21 / 3**

This day says that creativity, expression, and sensitivity will be the energies present. Social interaction is important, along with independence and ideals. The keyword is imagination.

# SEPTEMBER WEEK THREE - 15 THRU 21

**9 / 15 / 2023 = MASTER NUMBER 22**

This day says that structure and stability are being offered not only to your close circle but to everyone, Master potential is present. This number speaks to the need for a strong foundation. The keyword is commitment.

**9 / 16 / 2023 = 23 / 5**

This day says that physical activity, change, and excesses are the energies you will see. Being undecided will make you feel blocked or scattered, so make up your mind. The keyword is have faith in you.

**9 / 17 / 2023 = 24 / 6**

This day says that responsibility, love, and service to others are the energies you will see. Try to work toward a solid goal, and always use tact and logic. The keyword is

**9 / 18 / 2023 = 25 / 7**

This day says that spiritual, analytical, and skeptical are the mix of energies available. Such a potpourri, avoid questioning your faith or being overly cynical. The keyword is dynamic interaction.

**9 / 19 / 2023 = 26 / 8**

This day says that power, authority, and management skills are the energies prominent here. Issues with balance and commitment are also present. The keyword is impulsive.

**9 / 20 / 2023 = 18/ 9**

This day says that compassion, wisdom, and charity are the energies here. What will be important is independence and power. The keyword is tact.

**9 / 21 / 2023 = 19 / 10 / 1**

This day says that innovation, inventiveness, and ideals are in the works. It may be time to welcome changes as they are needed. Show your vision and assertiveness to all. The keyword is communication.

# SEPTEMBER WEEK FOUR - 22 THRU 28

**9 / 22 / 2023 = 38 / MASTER NUMBER 11**

This day says that the Master Teacher energy is present, people will seek your advice because your words hold power and truth. Always be careful of your balance. The keyword is building.

**9 / 23 / 2023 = 21 / 3**

This day says that communication, social situations, and action will be the most prominent. Feeling blocked, scattered, or just generally reserved may also need attention. The keyword is change.

**9 / 24 / 2023 = MASTER NUMBER 22**

This day says that the Master potential is present in the Master Builder bringing energies that will influence the many instead of the few. Maintaining your balance will be vital to hold this Master vibe. The keyword is love.

**9 / 25 / 2023 = 23 / 5**

This day says that physical activity, excesses, and random change will all be present energy-wise. Avoid restraint or restlessness.

The keyword is faith.

**9 / 26 / 2023 = 24 / 6**

This day says that commitment, love, and service to others are the energies present. Try not to entertain lower vibes like uncaring or irresponsibility. Take commitment seriously. The keyword is power.

**9 / 27 / 2023 = 25 / 7**

This day says that trust, spirituality, and faith are strong energies showing their presents. Try not to get judgmental or selfish because those feelings take away energy instead of adding it. The keyword is generosity.

**9 / 28 / 2023 = 26 / 8**

This day says that authority, management, and administrative skills are in play. Too much commitment will take a toll so delegate power to others. The keyword is innovation.

# SEPTEMBER WEEK FIVE - 29 THRU 30

**9 / 29 / 2023 = 27 / 9**

This day says that ancient innate wisdom, charity, and compassion are on tap energy-wise. Carrying ancient wisdom and being able to tap into it is special, know that. The keyword is teach.

**9 / 30 / 2023 = 19 / 10 / 1**

This day says that it may be time to share your foresight, and vision and welcome innovation. Put the modest insecure you away and declare yourself. The keyword is action.

# 2023 OCTOBER

This is a 10 month, which says that the energy is about fresh starts, taking chances on the unknown, and new beginnings. Pay attention to what has closed recently but try not to miss new opportunities opening up for you. Innovation and inventiveness will show activity this month. Work at bringing what you want to you, manifest by seeing it, knowing it is yours, and welcoming it to your life with open arms. As you see it. So be it.

# OCTOBER WEEK ONE
# - 1 THRU 7

**10 / 1 / 2023 = 9**

This day says that impulse, charity, and compassion are the energies you will feel most. Avoid the lower vibrations of jealousy or revenge. The keyword is ideals.

**10 / 2 / 2023 = 10 / 1**

This day says that bold ventures, new starts, and fresh enterprises will all be available energy-wise, take advantage. Seeds previously sown may be bearing fruit. The keyword is balance.

**10 / 3 / 2023 = MASTER NUMBER 11**

This day says that your balance and centering are the focus, Master Number 11 is putting pressure on you to speak your truth. Be careful to guard your independence. The keyword is socializing.

**10 / 4 / 2023 = 12 / 3**

This day says that sensitivity, creativity, and self-expression are energies that help to highlight the real you. Stand on your own two feet and take care with your balance. The keyword is work.

**10 / 5 / 2023 = 13 / 4**

This day says that work, obsessions, and chaos will be present. Do not let your stubborn side show, try regaining some order. The keyword is restless.

**10 / 6 / 2023 = 14 / 5**

This day says that freedom, physical activity, and moderation will rule the energies. Feeling insecure or unstable may haunt you, center yourself and go on. The keyword is tenacity.

**10 / 7 / 2023 = 15 / 6**

This day says that commitment, service, and responsibility will be in the mix energy-wise. Obstinance is seen as uncaring, or noncommittal to avoid this lower vibe. The keyword is spirituality.

# OCTOBER WEEK TWO - 8 THRU 14

**10 / 8 / 2023 = 16 / 7**

This day says that being well informed, having faith, and trusting is important. Try not to appear uncaring or non committal. The keyword is power.

**10 / 9 / 2023 = 17 / 8**

This day says that authority, management, and administrative skills are the energies to look for. Cynicism or lack of faith will derail positive efforts. The keyword is impulsive.

**10 / 10 / 2023 = 9**

This day says that compassion, altruism, and impulse are the energies at work here. if you are asking "what's in it for me?", then we need to talk about altruism. The keyword is individual.

**10 / 11 / 2023 = 19 / 10 / 1**

This day says that independence, innovation, and ideals will be the energies at play here. No room for modesty or insecurity, stand on your own and rule the day. The keyword is mentor.

## 10 / 12 / 2023 = MASTER NUMBER 11

This day says that the Master Teacher energy is present, people will heed your words and seek your advice as a knowledgeable individual. Choose your words wisely people are listening. The keyword is communication.

## 10 / 13 / 2023 = 12 / 3

This day says that communication, feelings, and self-expression are all paramount. Independence and balance will become important, and staying centered will help. The keyword is transition.

## 10 / 14 / 2023 = 13 / 4

This day says that work, organization, structure, and stability are what will present looking for attention. See what needs doing and do it, there is no discussion necessary to do what is needed. The keyword is freedom.

# OCTOBER WEEK THREE
# - 15 THRU 21

**10 / 15 / 2023 = 14 / 5**

This day says that imagination, adventure, and change will be in the mix of energies. See things as you want them to be. Try not to avoid things that appear different, take a chance, and try them. The keyword is responsibility.

**10 / 16 / 2023 = 15 / 6**

This day says that responsibility and tenacity are presenting themselves. Look out for infatuation, restlessness, or feeling moody. The keyword is faith.

**10 / 17 / 2023 = 16 / 7**

This day says that knowledge, introspection, and trusting self are what need to be addressed. Look within and trust what you see. You are strong and resourceful do not be derailed by love. The keyword is power.

**10 / 18 / 2023 = 17 / 8**

This day says that management, authority, and power will be in the mix. If asked to trust, do so, just don't do it  blindly always verify. The keyword is wisdom.

## 10 / 19 / 2023 = 18 / 9

This day says that charity, dynamics, and compassion will present themselves for attention. Do not judge or be resentful, these are lower vibrations and should be avoided. The keyword is compassion.

## 10 / 20 / 2023 = 10 / 1

This day says that ideals, innovation, and inventiveness will stand up and be heard. A strong ego with a forceful  nature may be present for you to deal with. The keyword is tact.

## 10 / 21 / 2023 = MASTER NUMBER 11

This day says that the Master Teacher is in the building. Your words will have an impact on others. Be on the alert for new beginnings, fresh starts, or do-overs of any kind. The keyword is creativity.

# OCTOBER WEEK FOUR - 22 THRU 28

**10 / 22 / 2023 = 30 / 3**

This day says that expression, creativity, and sensitivity are in the mix of energy we will see. We create our own reality so create what you want. The keyword is organization.

**10 / 23 / 2023 = 13 / 4**

This day says that organization, structure, and practicality are the prominent energies at work. Avoid engaging your sometimes obsessive nature is a path to chaos. The keyword is freedom.

**10 / 24 / 2023 = 14 / 5**

This day says that personal freedom, physical activity, and random change are all on board. Be practical and let the well-organized part of you take the lead. The keyword is responsibility.

**10 / 25 / 2023 = 15 / 6**

This day says that commitment, responsibility, and service to others will be in the mix energy-wise. Restlessness and irritability are subconscious lower vibrations and should be avoided. The keyword is spirituality.

**10 / 26 / 2023 = 16 / 7**

This day says that faith, trust, and spirituality are strong energies here. Stay connected to those who matter most and stay away from any idle commitments. The keyword is authority.

**10 / 27 / 2023 = 17 / 8**

This day says that money, power, and management are the focus. Managing time, money and people will show the world your power. Be careful whom you trust. The keyword is wisdom.

**10 / 28 / 202V3 = 18 / 9**

This day says that compassion, generosity, and impulse are the energies at work here. Independence and personal power will also be vying for attention. The keyword is new beginnings.

# OCTOBER WEEK FIVE
# - 29 THRU 31

**10 / 29 / 2023 = 19 / 10 / 1**

This day says that innovation, inventiveness, and ideals are in the works. You can sometimes be insecure or resentful. It could be time for a new start The keyword is influence.

**10 / 30 / 2023 = MASTER NUMBER 11**

This day says that being centered and balanced will be the focus. Master Number 11 is pressuring you to stand on your own and speak your truth. The keyword is expression.

**10 / 31 / 2023 = 12 / 3**

This day says that social interaction, popularity, and expression may be on the table. Feeling restricted or scattered may crop up to derail your positive social efforts. The keyword is structure.

# 2023 NOVEMBER

This is an 11 Master Number month and brings the energy of the Master Teacher to the foreground The potential is high to affect more than just your close circle of friends and acquaintances with this master number. You may find yourself addressing small groups or large crowds, but your point will be made, and you will be heard. Above all else maintain your balance and stay centered which will allow you to stay grounded while carrying this higher vibration.

# NOVEMBER WEEK ONE – 1 THRU 7

**11 / 1 / 2023 = 19 / 10 / 1**

This day says that independence, innovation, and ideals will stand up and be heard. Beware of the compassionate impulsive soul or a powerful ego that may also be present. The keyword is independence.

**11 / 2 / 2023 = 20 / 2**

This day says that persuasion, tact, and balance are all involved here. Be sure not to be indecisive or shy when interacting with others. The keyword is partnership.

**11 / 3 / 2023 = 21 / 3**

This day says that communication, self-expression, and action are the energies at play. Not feeling yourself or feeling blocked may try to keep you down. Rally and be that DO-ER that everybody loves. The keyword is action.

**11 / 4 / 2023 = MASTER NUMBER 22**

This day says that the Master potential is present in the form of the Master Builder, time to bring order to the chaos. Lay a solid foundation and sever ties that no longer serve you. The keyword is organization.

**11 / 5 / 2023 = 23 / 5**

This day says that adventure, change, and excess are the most prominent energies at work. Explore the unknown, expect random changes, and do not overdo it. The keyword is adventure.

**11 / 6 / 2023 = 24 / 6**

This day says that determination, control, and love, are the engine leading the energy train. maintain your balance and bring order where you can. The keyword is care deeply.

**11 / 7 / 2023 = 25 / 7**

This day says that introspection, knowledge, and faith will be important factors to consider. Sarcasm and building walls are defensive tactics and do little to raise your vibrations. The keyword is knowledge.

# NOVEMBER WEEK TWO - 8 THRU 14

**11 / 8 / 2023 = 26 / 8**

This day says that karma, material things, and power are the energies working here. Sarcasm, and cynicism, do not serve you. If you feel a karmic tie, dispel it (see afterword) for good. The keyword is manifest.

**11 / 9 / 2023 = 27 / 9**

This day says that wisdom, charity, and compassion will all be in the mix energy-wise. Nurturing and faith will be important tools for you to use. The keyword is compassion.

**11 / 10 / 2023 = 19 / 10 / 1**

This day says that new beginnings, fresh starts, or a new venture may be present energy-wise. An entire spectrum is present, see what works for you. Seek a compassionate match. The keyword is take a chance..

**11 / 11 / 2023 = 29 / MASTER NUMBER 11**

This day says that the Master Teacher is in the building. Your words will have an impact, others will be listening. There are new beginnings on the horizon so be on the lookout. The keyword is teacher.

## 11 / 12 / 2023 = 21 / 3

This day says that popularity, social interaction, and expression may be on the table. Feeling blocked or scattered may crop up to derail your positive social efforts. The keyword is sensitivity.

## 11 / 13 / 2023 = MASTER NUMBER 22

This day says that the Master Builder in you can bring order to chaotic situations. Use this potential while it is present. Avoid emotional outbursts, being deceptive, or shy. The keyword is structure.

## 11 / 14 / 2023 = 23 / 5

This day says that moderation, random change, and physical activity will all be present energy-wise. Avoid restlessness, excesses, or restraints. The keyword is imagination.

# NOVEMBER WEEK THREE - 15 THRU 21

**11 / 15 / 2023 = 24 / 6**

This day says that responsibility, commitment, and service to others are the energies present. Take commitment seriously and avoid lower vibrations like being uncaring or irresponsible. The keyword is love.

**11 / 16 / 2023 = 25 / 7**

This day says that spirituality, faith, and trust are the strongest energies shown here. Stay centered and take care to avoid excessive behavior or restlessness. The keyword is knowledge

**11 / 17 / 2023 = 26 / 8**

This day says that authority, management, and material concerns are in play. Too much commitment will take a toll so you may want to delegate power to others. The keyword is more money.

**11 / 18 / 2023 = 27 / 9**

This day says that compassion, charity, and innate wisdom, are the energies at work here. Shyness, indecision,  along with a loss of faith may appear. These are lower vibrations, take measures to transmute them. The keyword is generosity.

**11 / 19 / 2023 = 28 / 10 / 1**

This day says that independence, standing on your own, and speaking your truth will be important. Be on the lookout for that new beginning or fresh start while maintain your balance. The keyword is visionary.

**11 / 20 / 2023 = 20 / 2**

This day says that balance, tact, and emotion are the energies most at play. Be careful not to wear your emotions on your sleeve or allow yourself to be victimized. Just maintaining your balance. The keyword is nurture those around you.

**11 / 21 / 2023 = 21 / 3**

This day says that taking action, self-expression, and  sensitivity are the energies at play. With so much activity in the cosmos, you may be feeling out of sorts or blocked. The keyword is creativity.

# NOVEMBER WEEK FOUR - 22 THRU 28

**11 / 22 / 2023 = 40 / 4**

This day says that work, stability, and organization will be present energy-wise. You will be focusing on work, do what you have to. There is also master potential here. The keyword is build.

**11 / 23 / 2023 = 23 / 5**

This day says that freedom, change, and excesses are the energies looking for attention. Venture out, embrace the new, and avoid undue restraints. The keyword is adventurous.

**11 / 24 / 2023 = 24 / 6**

This day says that commitment, love, and service to others are the energies present. Try to avoid imbalance or instability, and not entertain lower vibrations like uncaring or irresponsibility. The keyword is commitment.

**11 / 25 / 2023 = 25 / 7**

This day says that trust, faith, and spirituality are strong energies showing their presents. Stay centered and try to see the adventure in life. The keyword is trust.

**11 / 26 / 2023 = 26 / 8**

This day says that power, material things, and karma are the energies working here. Put aside sarcasm, and cynicism, they do not serve you. If you feel a karmic tie, dispel it for good. (see afterword) The keyword is management.

**11 / 27 / 2023 = 27 / 9**

This day says that dynamics, compassion, and charity will present themselves for attention. Do not judge or be resentful, these lower vibrations should be avoided. The keyword is innate wisdom.

**11 / 28 / 2023 = 28 / 10 / 1**

This day says that it may be time to share your independent nature and your vision for the future with others. Welcome innovation. Put the modest insecure you away and declare yourself. The keyword is fresh start.

# NOVEMBER WEEK FIVE - 29 THRU 30

**11 / 29 / 2023 = 29 / MASTER NUMBER 11**

This day says that the Master Teacher is in the building. Your words will have an impact on those around you.  New beginnings are definitely coming so be on the lookout. The keyword is advise.

**11 / 30 / 2023 = 21 / 3**

This day says that communication, feelings, and self-expression will all be of paramount importance. Maintaining your balance and speaking your truth will help. The keyword is sensitivity.

# 2023 DECEMBER

This is a 3 month, which says that it is all about action, sensitivity, and creativity. Having great ideas and acting on those ideas are two very different things. At some point, we have to take action to move the idea into a plan so it can be executed properly. Sometimes it is socializing that stops us, or maybe just feel scattered or blocked. But mostly it is our sensitivity that holds us back because we feel every aspect of the progress. Learn to decern what those feelings are saying, so you can regroup faster. It is a process.

# DECEMBER WEEK ONE - 1 THRU 7

**12 / 1 / 2023 = MASTER NUMBER 11**


This day says that the Master Teacher energy is present, people will heed your words, seek your advice and value your knowledge. The keyword is ideals.


**12 / 2 / 2023 = 12 / 3**


This day says that sensitivity, creativity, and self-expression are energies that help to show the real you to the rest of the world. stay independent and in balance, which will enhance everything else. The keyword is tact.


**12 / 3 / 2023 = 13 / 4**


This day says that obsessions, work, and chaos will be present. You may feel blocked, do not let yourself get scattered or hold back. Try to regain some order that will help put things right again. The keyword is creativity.


**12 / 4 / 2023 = 14 / 5**


This day says that imagination, adventure, and change will be in the mix of energies. In your mind's eye see things as you want them to be. Seek out things that are different and try them. The keyword is practical.

## 12 / 5 / 2023 = 15 / 6

This day says that love, determination, and control are the energies most prominent. Assert your independence and try not to become restless. The keyword is freedom.

## 12 / 6 / 2023 = 16 / 7

This day says that faith, knowledge, and trust are leading the energies at play. You may be haveing to define your spirituality. Know your truth and trust your insight, and the right answer is there. The keyword is love.

## 12 / 7 / 2023 = 17 / 8

This day says that authority, management, and power will be in the mix. You may be asked to trust but do not do that blindly, always verify. The keyword is spirituality.

# DECEMBER WEEK TWO - 8 THRU 14

**12 / 8 / 2023 = 18 / 9**

This day says that ancient innate wisdom, charity, and compassion are on tap energy-wise Manage your resources and maintain your independence. The keyword is authority.

**12 / 9 / 2023 = 19 / 10 / 1**

This day says that new starts, bold ventures, and fresh enterprises will all be available energy-wise, take advantage. The full spectrum of possibilities is spread before you. The keyword is wisdom.

**12 / 10 / 2023 = MASTER NUMBER 11**

This day says that everything is raised to a higher level, balance, tact, learning, and advice. Be careful to stand your ground and speak your truth because others are listening. The keyword is new venture.

**12 / 11 / 2023 = 21 / 3**

This day says that action, communication, and social situations will be the most prominent. Feeling blocked, scattered, or just generally reserved may also need attention. The keyword is advisor.

**12 / 12 / 2023 = 31 / 4**

This day says that work, obsessions, and chaos will be present. self-expression and creativity may be stifled. Try reinforcing the structure and moving forward with your  plans. The keyword is expression.

**12 / 13 / 2023 = 14 / 5**

This day says that physical activity, personal freedom, and random change are all on board. Stability and independence may be challenged. The keyword is work

**12 / 14 / 2023 = 15 / 6**

This day says that infatuation, responsibility, and tenacity are presenting themselves. Avoid being restless, excessive, and moody because those are lower vibes. The keyword is physical activity.

# DECEMBER WEEK
# THREE - 15 THRU 21

**12 / 15 / 2023 = 16 / 7**

This day says that being well informed, having faith, and trusting will be of importance. Value your ideals, love with an open heart, and listen to your inner voice. The keyword is caring.

**12 / 16 / 2023 = 17 / 8**

This day says that management, administrative skills, and authority are in play. This may be a time to trust someone else with some of your power and delegate. The keyword is introspection.

**12 / 17 / 2023 = 18 / 9**

This day says that charity, altruism, and compassion are the energies at work here. Beware of the lower vibrations of insecurity or revenge. The keyword is authority.

**12 / 18 / 2023 = 19 / 10 / 1**

This day says that independence, standing on your own, and speaking your truth will be important. Keep your eyes open for the new, the fresh, or just the different, and maintain your balance. The keyword is charity.

**12 / 19 / 2023 = 20 / 2**

This day says that persuasion, tact, and balance are all involved here. Be sure not to be shy or emotional when interacting with others. The keyword is innovative.

**12 / 20 / 2023 = 12 / 3**

This day says that communication, feelings, and self-expression are all paramount. Always value your independence, maintain your balance, and stay centered. The keyword is nurtured.

**12 / 21 / 2023 = 13 / 4**

This day says that work, structure, and organization will be present. Do not wear your sensitive side on your sleeve, but try to express your true self. The keyword is action.

# DECEMBER WEEK FOUR - 22 THRU 28

**12 / 22 / 2023 = 32 / 5**

This day says that imagination, adventure, and moderation will be in the mix. Be excited to see what is coming and exercise moderation in all activities. The keyword is order.

**12 / 23 / 2023 = 15 / 6**

This day says that determination, control, and love are the energies most prominent. Assert your independence and do not overdo it. The keyword is imagination.

**12 / 24 / 2023 = 16 / 7**

This day says that analytics, sarcasm, and being cynical are energies you may see or feel. There is too much happening, slow down and regroup. Listen to happy music, walk on the earth, or center yourself. The keyword is love.

**12 / 25 / 2023 = 17 / 8**

This day says that money, power, and management are the focus. Managing time, money and people will establish your power. Be careful whom you trust. The keyword is introspection.

**12 / 26 / 2023 = 18 / 9**

This day says that compassion, wisdom, and charity are the energies here. What will be important is independence and authority.  The keyword is power.

**12 / 27 / 2023 = 19 /10 / 1**

This day says that taking chances, standing on your own, and starting new are the prominent things. Try not to be impulsive or selfish. The keyword is charity.

**12 / 28 / 2023 = 20 / 2**

This day says that balance, tact, and nurturing are the energies most at play. Be careful not to be too emotional it could lead to being victimized. Just maintain your balance. The keyword is independence.

# DECEMBER WEEK FIVE
# - 29 THRU 31

**12 / 29 / 2023 = 21 / 3**

This day says that expression, creativity, and sensitivity are in the mix of energy we will see. Create what you want, express yourself wisely, and stay in balance. The keyword is teacher.

**12 / 30 / 2023 = 13 / 4**

This day says that structure, organization, and work will have an influence energy-wise. Take care in how you express yourself, your sensitive side may be showing. The keyword is communication.

**12 / 31 / 2023 = 14 / 5**

This day says that physical activity, change, and personal freedom are at the forefront. Pay special attention at work, things may be chaotic, and try not to show that stubborn side. The keyword is organize.

# ABOUT THE AUTHOR

## Deborah Breeland

Deborah Breeland has been a practicing Numerologist for over 50 years, with clients all over the world. Creator of the NUMERIC HARMONY CARDS, an insightful divination tool based on numerology, and author of 'NUMERIC HARMONY – Numerology Simplified' a book based on the same system.

As a Psychic, Reiki Master. Intuitive, and Healer, she uses her abilities to give personal insight and guidance with your growth and help overcome obstacles along your path. Either with a Numerology Chart, the Daily NUMBERSCOPE, or a reading from the Numeric Harmony Card deck

On Facebook, I am still posting my daily NUMBERSCOPE to a few different pages. On Facebook look for #dailynumericharmony or #numberscope. Follow me on Facebook @Deborah Breeland, to get the NUMBERSCOPE daily, as I post them.

# BOOKS BY THIS AUTHOR

**Numeric Harmony - Numerology Simplified**

Explore the deeper meaning of your life that can be obtained from the numbers that represent you. It is available to you in your given name, birth date, and other significant numbers in your life.

Numeric Harmony can reveal hidden secrets and motivations that have led you to where you are now. It can help you live your purpose, fulfill your heart's desire, unleash your intuition, or make big choices with ease and confidence. By looking at these things you can better understand yourself, therefore, a better understanding of others.

# AFTERWORD

Many of this year's NUMBERSCOPES referred to karma. Karma is the engine that drives some of our action's life after life. It is based on the universal law, "What goes around comes around". In other words, it is " If you kicked my cat in another life, I am going to kick your dog in this life."

And so it goes, incarnation after incarnation until it is boiled down to just an internal discomfort that affects the way we act toward those to which we are karmically tied. In most cases, we are not even aware of WHY we feel the way we do.

Here is a helpful exercise that anyone can use. I came across this technique while listening to a channeling by Lee Carroll, the original KRYON channel. I pass it along to anyone interested in not being controlled by forces set in motion sometimes eons ago.

# KARMA

## How to eliminate it

There have been many changes recently with the thinning of the veil, and the massive energy influx that we have all been experiencing. It has become known that we all possess more personal power than we ever have in the past. One of the things that we are now capable of is transmuting and dispelling karma forever.

Karma is the engine that helps to drive our actions and reactions in one incarnation after another, sometimes for centuries. We all have the power and ability to stop this process in its tracks, with just a few simple steps. It just takes pulling upon the knowledge that we carry, trusting that the knowledge is accurate, and giving our intent to transmute and dispel our karmic energy for all time.

**Step 1.** Acknowledge that you have a karmic situation at play in your life.

**Step 2.** Forgive everyone involved (including YOURSELF), for whatever part was played in this drama. For instance, you kicked my cat, so I am going to kick your dog, and so it starts. Until it gets to a place where you do not even know how it originally started, who did what first, and to whom, but in reality, that does not matter.

**Step 3.** Visualize the karmic energy as a sphere that you are infusing with light, love, and understanding. That energy will gradually get lighter and lose the density that it carried when it could influence you.

**Step 4.** Send that transmuted energy sphere back to the universe to be dispelled forever. You have transmuted it so sending it away from you is as easy as seeing it as a helium balloon and releasing it to float harmlessly into the sky until it disappears.

Another way is to use an energy-moving technique like Reiki to move the transmuted energy. These are the techniques that I am aware of and have used, but whatever way that spirit moves you, is the right way to do it. Once completed, and you have successfully transmuted and dispersed the energy, your karma is gone forever.

Offered With Love and Warmth.
Deborah Breeland